CLASSIFIED

D0126041

REVOLUTIONARY WAR

BY NEL YOMTOV

Consultant:
Jan Goldman, EdD
Founding Board Member
International Intelligence Ethics Association
Washington, D.C.

CAPSTONE PRESS
a capstone imprint

Velocity Books are published by Capstone Press,
1710 Roe Crest Drive, North Mankato, Minnesota 56003
www.capstonepub.com

Library of Congress Cataloging-in-Publication Data
Yomtov, Nelson.
Revolutionary war spies / by Nel Yomtov.
pages cm. — (Classified)
Includes bibliographical references and index.
Summary: "Describes the dangerous missions of several Revolutionary War spies"—
Provided by publisher.
ISBN 978-1-4296-9977-8 (library binding)
ISBN 978-1-4765-3585-2 (ebook pdf)
1. United States—History—Revolution, 1775-1783—Secret service—Juvenile literature. 2.
Spies—United States—History—18th century. I. Title.
E279.Y66 2014
973.3'85—dc23   2013009489

Editorial Credits
Mandy Robbins, editor; Veronica Scott, designer; Jennifer Walker, production specialist

Photo Credits
Alamy: Mary Evans Picture Library, 9, North Wind Picture Archives, 14, 18-19, 31, 36, 40,
World History Archive, 44-45; Corbis, 5, 43, Bettmann, 17, 34; CriaImages.com: Jay Robert
Nash Collection, 15; Getty Images: Hulton Archive, 33, MPI, 20; iStockphotos: Maher, 8;
Landov: Ivy Close Images, 22, 38 (inset); Library of Congress, 23, 27, 28; National Archives
and Records Administration, 16; Newscom: Everett Collection, 12-13; Shutterstock: B Brown,
24-25, Balefire, 38-39, bkp, cover (cannon), Evlakhov Valeriy, 26, I. Pilon, 6, 40-41, Iwona
Grodzka, 37, Jason L. Price, 11, Ken Cave, 10 (money), luchschen, 10-11, Victorian Traditions,
7, Wutthichai, cover (stone pavement); The Granger Collection, NYC, 29

Artistic Effects
Shutterstock

Direct Quotes
p. 12 from "Letter from Issac Ketham to the New-York Congress: Has important matters to
communicate; Hickey and Lynch have informed him of the conspiracy " located at http://
lincoln.lib.niu.edu/cgi-bin/philologic/getobject.pl?c.17194:1.amarch

p. 37 from "The Connecticut Society of the Sons of the American Revolution" http://www.
connecticutsar.org/patriots/hale_nathan_2.htm

Printed in the United States of America in Stevens Point, Wisconsin.
012014   007959R

TABLE OF CONTENTS

INTRODUCTION
SPIES OF THE REVOLUTION 4

ISAAC KETCHAM
CRIMINAL SPY 8

BENEDICT ARNOLD
AMERICAN TRAITOR 16

LYDIA DARRAGH
QUAKER SPY 22

NATHAN HALE
ONE LIFE TO LOSE 30

ANN BATES
SUCCESSFUL LOYALIST SPY 38

CONCLUSION
BIRTH OF A NATION 44

GLOSSARY 46

READ MORE 47

INTERNET SITES 47

INDEX 48

SPIES OF THE REVOLUTION

Before and during the Revolutionary War (1775–1783), American **colonists** carried out a rebellion under the watchful eyes of the British. The colonists struggled to break free from Great Britain's rule. It was clear that Great Britain would not let the colonies go without a fight. Both sides needed accurate information about their enemies' actions. This is where spies came in.

ROOTS OF REBELLION

The American Revolution happened after about 150 years of British settlement in North America. In the early 1600s, England began forming colonies in North America. By 1773 there were 13 colonies along North America's eastern coast. The British government ruled the colonies and fought wars to protect them.

In 1754 England went to war with France for control of more land in North America. The British won the war, but at a high cost.

To raise money after the war, the British government put new taxes on the Americans. The colonists thought the taxes were unfair because they were not represented in the British government. Many colonists, called Patriots, wanted to break free from British rule. Another group of colonists, called Loyalists, were loyal to the British government.

As time passed, tension between Great Britain and the colonists grew. Eventually war could not be avoided. In April 1775, the first shots of the American Revolutionary War were fired at the towns of Lexington and Concord in Massachusetts.

The British and the Patriots fired at each other at a bridge in Concord, Massachusetts.

colonist—a person who settles in a new territory that is governed by his or her home country, the settled area is called a colony

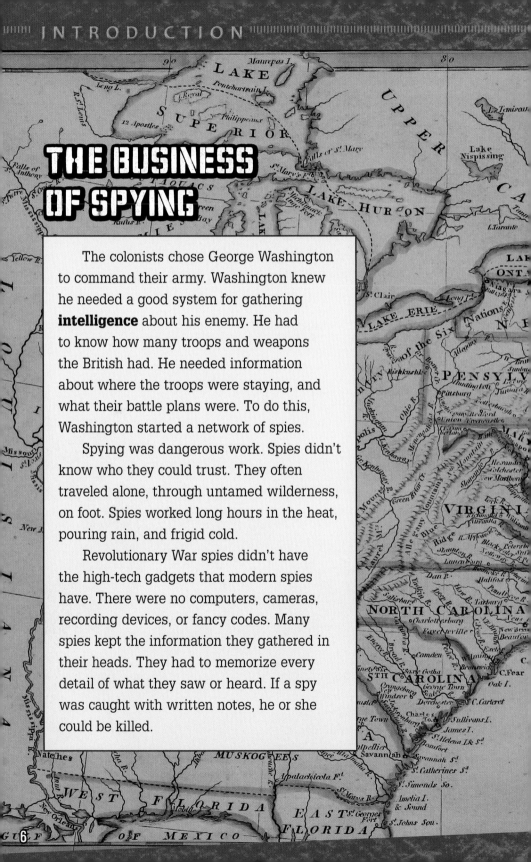

THE BUSINESS OF SPYING

The colonists chose George Washington to command their army. Washington knew he needed a good system for gathering **intelligence** about his enemy. He had to know how many troops and weapons the British had. He needed information about where the troops were staying, and what their battle plans were. To do this, Washington started a network of spies.

Spying was dangerous work. Spies didn't know who they could trust. They often traveled alone, through untamed wilderness, on foot. Spies worked long hours in the heat, pouring rain, and frigid cold.

Revolutionary War spies didn't have the high-tech gadgets that modern spies have. There were no computers, cameras, recording devices, or fancy codes. Many spies kept the information they gathered in their heads. They had to memorize every detail of what they saw or heard. If a spy was caught with written notes, he or she could be killed.

George Washington

intelligence—information that can be used to help defeat an enemy

CRIMINAL SPY

One of the oddest stories of **espionage** during the Revolutionary War involved a criminal. The spy's name was Isaac Ketcham. But Ketcham may never have become a spy if it weren't for Henry Dawkins.

Dawkins was an artist and **engraver** who made maps for the wealthy people of Philadelphia. In early January 1776, he was put in a New York City jail for making **counterfeit** money. When he was released a few weeks later, Dawkins headed to Long Island, east of New York. There he stayed at the house of two brothers, Israel and Isaac Youngs.

Dawkins convinced Israel Youngs to help him buy a printing press. Dawkins told him that he could make a lot of money printing labels for the hat industry. But Dawkins' real intention was to use the press to make counterfeit money again. He set up the press in the Youngs' attic. In those days, counterfeiting money wasn't difficult to do. But Dawkins needed the right kind of paper. For that, he turned to Isaac Ketcham.

In colonial days, each state had its own money.

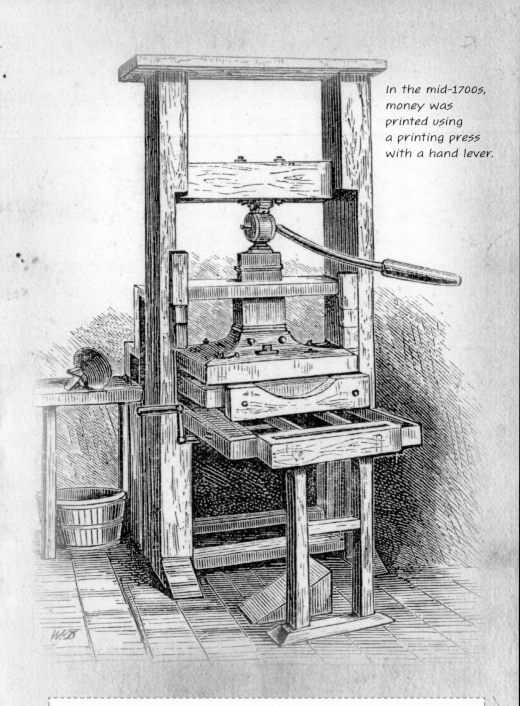

In the mid-1700s, money was printed using a printing press with a hand lever.

espionage—the actions of a spy to gain sensitive information
engraver—someone who cuts a design or writing into a metal or other hard surface
counterfeit—fake, but looking like the real thing

Ketcham got a sample of the paper Dawkins wanted. He went to Philadelphia to get prices for buying a batch of it. Someone got suspicious of Ketcham, and he was arrested. Then Henry Dawkins foolishly told someone about his plans, and he too was arrested. To top it off, the Youngs brothers were arrested too.

The four men were jailed for attempted counterfeit, which was a minor crime. Their cell mates included Loyalists. Ketcham overheard some Loyalists talking about plans to destroy the colonists' fight for freedom. He hoped to bargain his way out of prison by trading what he overheard for his freedom. Ketcham decided he would spy on the Loyalists.

While talking with them, Ketcham learned of at least two plans. The first was to kidnap General Washington and his guards. The second was for Loyalist troops to attack the Americans in weak spots in their army's locations. While doing that, Loyalists would also blow up Patriot ammunition storage sites and take American cannons. They would then fire on the Patriots with their own guns.

Ketcham was no military expert, but he thought the plots had a chance to succeed. The Loyalists were well armed and organized. British ships could easily land troops, weapons, and supplies. Without a strong navy to guard its shores, the Americans could do little to stop Britain's Royal Navy.

In early June 1776, Ketcham wrote a note to the Provincial Congress of New York. He asked to be released from jail, claiming he was full of "shame and confusion for his past misconduct." Ketcham also appealed to the kindness of the congressmen, begging to be released so that he could care for his "six poor children."

Ketcham followed up his first note a week later by writing that he had something important to tell them. The Congressional leader met with Ketcham to learn the information. He told Ketcham that if he could gather more specific information about the Loyalists' plans, he would be freed. If not, he would remain in jail. Ketcham agreed to the offer and returned to the jail as a government spy.

The British Navy used Boston's harbor to transport soldiers, weapons, and supplies.

George Washington
greeting citizens of
Cambridge, Massachusetts

Back in jail, Ketcham picked up more information about the plots. He met Sergeant Thomas Hickey and Private Michael Lynch, two of Washington's former guards. The men had been jailed for using counterfeit bills. Hickey foolishly bragged that he was involved in Loyalist plots. Ketcham spent days pumping Hickey and Lynch for further information. He then sent a note to Congress saying he had discovered which men were involved in the plots he had learned of earlier.

New York authorities then learned more about the plots from other sources. The plotters included three other soldiers from Washington's guard and the New York City mayor, David Matthews. Arrests were quickly made. As promised, Ketcham was released from jail.

FACT:
Hickey was hanged, but there are no records to explain what happened to the others involved in Hickey's plot. Twenty thousand people witnessed Hickey's hanging.

AMERICAN TRAITOR

One of America's greatest war heroes was also one of its most hated **traitors**. His name was Benedict Arnold.

Arnold joined the Continental Army when war broke out in 1775. He helped capture Fort Ticonderoga from the British that year. In 1777, as a Major General, Arnold was the hero at the Battle of Saratoga. That battle turned the war in the colonists' favor.

Washington admired and trusted Arnold. But many fellow officers found him to be impatient and rude. Arnold was also accused of using military personnel for personal favors. Because of this, Arnold was passed over for a promotion. Arnold felt disrespected and underpaid.

Benedict Arnold

traitor—a person who helps the enemy of his or her country

Benedict Arnold (center) was shot in the leg at the Battle of Saratoga.

Arnold and his wife, Margaret "Peggy" Shippen, lived in Philadelphia. There Arnold also served as military governor. The couple lived in a fine home, wore elegant clothing, and hosted fancy parties. Unfortunately, Arnold didn't have the money to pay for these luxuries. Peggy wanted a grand lifestyle. Arnold's lack of funds made her very unhappy.

In spring 1779, Arnold contacted the British without revealing his identity. He offered to provide them with valuable information about American troops. In return, he wanted to be paid handsomely. Through secret letters, he worked out a deal with John André, the chief British intelligence officer. To prove his worth, Arnold gave the British information about an American naval landing at Newport, Rhode Island.

Arnold and André used two secret inks to write messages. One type of ink became visible by heat. The other appeared with a special acid that was applied to the writing. They also used a "dictionary code," in which numbers gave the page, the column, and the word they wanted to use taken from two books.

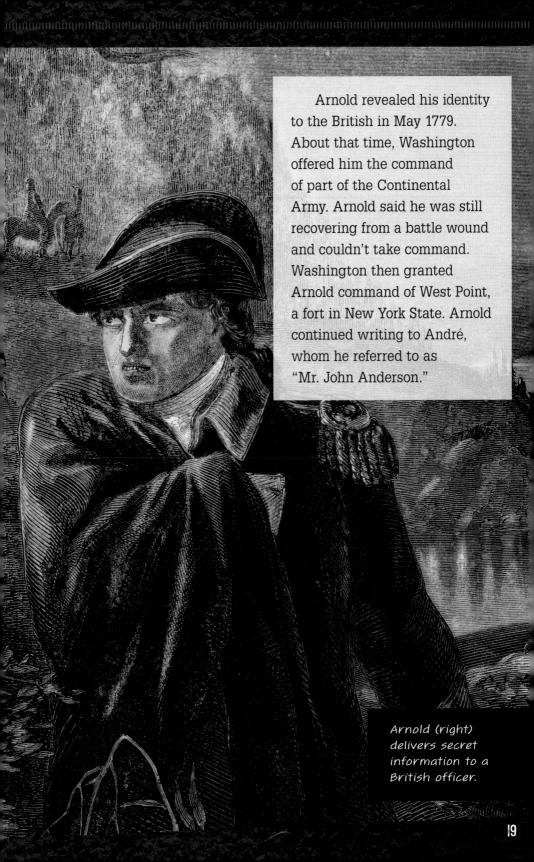

Arnold revealed his identity to the British in May 1779. About that time, Washington offered him the command of part of the Continental Army. Arnold said he was still recovering from a battle wound and couldn't take command. Washington then granted Arnold command of West Point, a fort in New York State. Arnold continued writing to André, whom he referred to as "Mr. John Anderson."

Arnold (right) delivers secret information to a British officer.

Once in command at West Point, Arnold scattered his troops, making the fort almost defenseless. Then he gave André information and maps to help the British capture the fort. Arnold also gave André a signed pass that would allow him to travel safely as he spied in Patriot territories.

an artist's depiction of the capture of John André

DISCRIPTION OF DEFENCES. ORDNANCE. WEST POINT.

PLAN OF WEST POINT.

Lith. & Pub. by N. Currier

WILLIAMS.   VAN WART.

CAPTURE   OF   AN

treason—the crime of betraying one's country

of the Southern District of N. Y.

PAULDING.

E 1780 **FACT?**

Three Patriot soldiers approached André on his way back to the British lines. They found the notes and maps André was carrying and turned him over to a nearby Continental Army camp.

The commanding officer sent a messenger to Arnold. The messenger told him that a spy had been found with a fake pass. Instantly Arnold knew André had been caught. It would be only a matter of time before Arnold's part in the **treason** would be discovered.

Arnold left his house and headed to a boat docked on the nearby Hudson River. He was taken to the British ship, the *Vulture*. It had been waiting to pick up André. Arnold was quickly whisked to the protection of the British. He was never punished for his crimes against his own country. André, on the other hand, was hanged as a spy in 1780.

QUAKER SPY

Lydia Darragh lived with her family in Philadelphia in 1777. At the time, the British controlled the city. British general William Howe was stationed near the Darragh's home in a townhouse he had taken over for his headquarters. The Darraghs were Quakers, a Christian group that opposed war. Lydia's son, Charles, had joined the Continental Army, despite his parents' opposition to war. He was stationed with Washington at Whitemarsh, the army's winter camp. The camp was about 8 miles (13 km) from Philadelphia.

According to Darragh family history, Lydia was running her own **spy ring**. When Howe and his officers met at his headquarters, Lydia watched their comings and goings. She wrote what she saw in code on small pieces of paper. Lydia then sewed the notes into the cloth jacket buttons of her 14-year-old son, John. The boy would walk to Whitemarsh to see his brother. Charles would cut off the buttons, decode the messages, and deliver them to his superior officers. The plan worked perfectly time and time again.

spy ring—a group of spies working together for a common goal

General Howe made the Darraghs let him use a large room in their home for meetings. On December 2, 1777, a British officer told Lydia to send her family to bed by 8:00 pm. The British officers were having an important meeting that evening.

Lydia couldn't sleep, so she slipped into a small closet next to the meeting room. She was stunned at what she overheard the officers say. In two days, the British would march out of Philadelphia and attack Washington's army at Whitemarsh.

Lydia rushed back to bed and pretended to be asleep. Suddenly, she was startled by a knock at her bedroom door. Then another. Finally, making herself look unusually sleepy, she answered the door. It was a British officer telling her that the meeting was over. He ordered her to lock up the house when they left.

a re-creation of a typical colonial bedroom

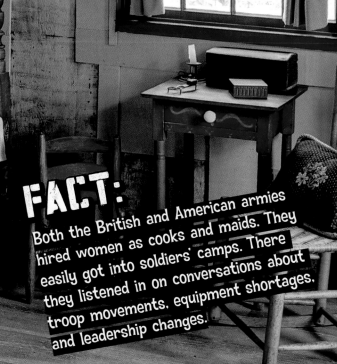

FACT:
Both the British and American armies hired women as cooks and maids. They easily got into soldiers' camps. There they listened in on conversations about troop movements, equipment shortages, and leadership changes.

Lydia knew she had to do something. But what? She decided not to tell her family anything about the British plans. The next day, she set out to get flour at a mill in Frankford. The mill was about 5 miles (8 km) away. Lydia grabbed an empty flour sack and got a pass from British headquarters. The pass would allow her to travel outside the city.

Plodding along a snow-covered road, Lydia dropped off the sack at the mill. She then turned toward the Continental camp at Whitemarsh. As she walked, Lydia met an officer in the Continental Army. Lydia told the officer what she had overheard the night before. Historians aren't sure if the officer went to Washington himself, or if he had a messenger go. But one thing is certain: Lydia's message made its way to Whitemarsh. Lydia turned back, picked up her bag of flour from the mill, and walked back to Philadelphia.

At midnight on December 4, the British Army marched out of Philadelphia toward Whitemarsh. British leaders thought they would surprise and crush the American troops. But the Continental Army had strengthened its positions. When the British were about to attack, the Americans were ready. Surprised by the Americans' preparedness, the British decided to turn back. The attack had failed. The British troops slumped back into Philadelphia.

Continental Army soldiers

Lydia Darragh is questioned by a British soldier.

The British knew there had been a leak somewhere. Lydia grew worried. Shortly after the British returned to Philadelphia, Lydia was summoned to their conference room. "Had anyone been awake in your house on the night the officers met?" an officer asked. "I need not ask you, because we had great difficulty waking you. But one thing is certain—the enemy had notice of our coming." "No, they were all in bed and asleep," she replied. With that, the officer stormed off.

Lydia's spying was never discovered. Her bravery helped the Continental Army escape disaster at Whitemarsh.

ONE LIFE TO LOSE

Nathan Hale was probably the most famous American spy of the Revolutionary War. He was also the least successful. Nathan was a graduate of Yale University and a schoolteacher in Connecticut.

In late August 1776, British forces defeated the Americans at the Battle of Long Island. After the defeat, General Washington moved his troops from Brooklyn, on Long Island, to New York City.

Washington wanted to find out how many British troops were on Long Island and what their movements were. He also needed to know about their supplies and weapons. Any amount of information could help his army retake the island. Washington ordered one of his commanders to find someone willing to go behind enemy lines as a spy.

Nathan Hale volunteered for the dangerous mission. Hale was a captain in the Continental Army, but he had no training as a spy. His mission was badly planned. He had no contact with Patriots living behind British lines. He also had no way of communicating with the Continental Army. Hale would have to write down everything he observed in notes that he carried. But he wasn't given any disappearing ink.

In early September, Hale left Manhattan and traveled by boat to Huntington, Long Island. He assumed the role of a schoolteacher looking for work. Several days into his mission, Hale learned that the British had invaded Manhattan. This bold move changed everything. If British general William Howe succeeded, he would move his men and supplies from Brooklyn to Manhattan. Hale would have nothing to spy on but empty campsites.

George Washington discusses Nathan Hale's mission with him.

Nathan Hale sneaks behind British lines disguised as a schoolteacher.

Hale did the only thing he could think to do. He hurried west almost 40 miles (64 km) to Brooklyn. Hale made sketches of British positions and took notes on the number and movement of British troops whenever he encountered them.

Hale made it to Manhattan. He went behind enemy lines and gathered intelligence on the British troops. Loaded with detailed information, he started making his way back to American lines.

On the night of September 21, however, Hale was arrested when crossing back to New York City. Most historians believe that he mistook a rowboat from a British warship for a Patriot boat sent to take him to the Americans.

Hale was doomed. The British found the maps and notes he was carrying. He admitted to being an officer in the Continental Army and a spy. Hale was taken to General Howe's Manhattan headquarters. Howe ordered Hale to be hanged without a trial.

Nathan Hale at his execution

The next morning, Hale was hanged. Just as the hangman's noose was about to be put around his neck, Hale uttered his famous last words. He said, "I only regret that I have but one life to lose for my country." Hale was 21 years old.

General Washington was greatly disturbed by the poor planning and bad decisions that led to Hale's death. Never again were such mistakes made by Washington or his spy network.

FACT:

A monument of Nathan Hale stands in his birthplace of Coventry, Connecticut.

SUCCESSFUL LOYALIST SPY

Sir Henry Clinton

Flintlock pistols were a common sidearm during the Revolutionary War.

George Washington wasn't the only Revolutionary War leader who had a network of spies. British commander Sir Henry Clinton also had one. Clinton's most successful spy was Ann Bates. She was a Loyalist schoolteacher from Philadelphia.

Ann was married to Joseph Bates. He was a weapons repairman in the British Army. In 1778 the British left Philadelphia and headed east toward New York. At that time, a Loyalist named John Cregge asked Ann to go see Sir Henry Clinton in New York. Clinton had a job for her.

Somehow, Ann talked Benedict Arnold, who was not yet a traitor, into giving her a pass to visit Washington's camp in New York. Armed with the pass, she traveled safely through New Jersey and arrived in New York in the summer of 1778.

Once in New York, Sir Henry Clinton's assistant gave Ann some money and a token. The token would identify her to a disloyal American officer secretly serving the British Army. Ann filled a pack with herbs, needles, combs, knives, and thread. Then she set off on her first spy mission. She played the role of a **peddler**.

peddler—a person who travels around selling things

In early July, Ann arrived at a Continental Army camp in White Plains, north of New York. There she sold her goods to American troops. As the wife of a weapons repairman, she was able to take detailed notes about the Americans' guns and cannons. She also met a trustworthy old friend in the camp. Ann got information from him about troop movements.

a Continental Army camp

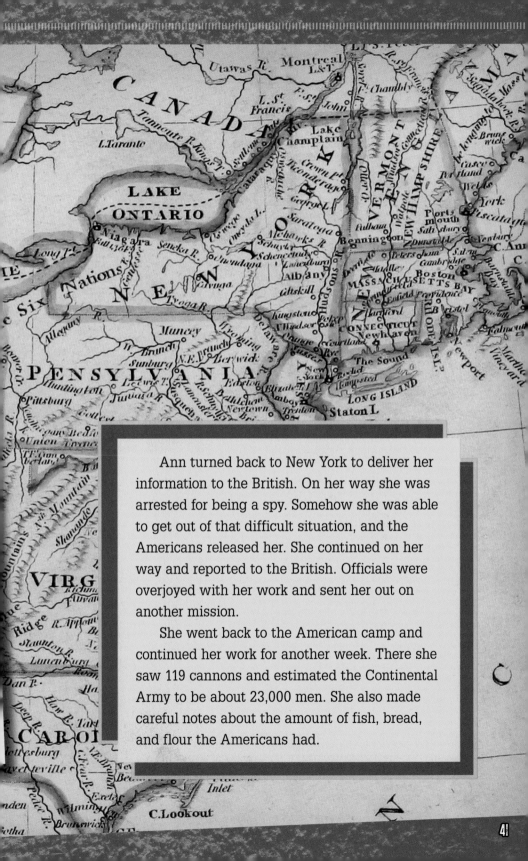

Ann turned back to New York to deliver her information to the British. On her way she was arrested for being a spy. Somehow she was able to get out of that difficult situation, and the Americans released her. She continued on her way and reported to the British. Officials were overjoyed with her work and sent her out on another mission.

She went back to the American camp and continued her work for another week. There she saw 119 cannons and estimated the Continental Army to be about 23,000 men. She also made careful notes about the amount of fish, bread, and flour the Americans had.

Ann continued her missions throughout July and August. Each time, she gathered information, returned to Clinton in New York, and then went back to the American camp.

In September Ann marched with the Continental Army to Connecticut. Washington had established a new headquarters there. Ann gathered information about the positions of American troops from New York to Connecticut.

Later in the month, it seemed Ann's luck had run out. She was captured in New York and questioned by American general Charles Scott. The quick-thinking Ann told him she was the wife of a soldier in one of the divisions that she had been spying on. Ann knew all the answers to the questions Scott asked her about that division. Scott gave a pass to the enemy's most dangerous spy!

Eventually, Ann told the British that she feared for her life and wanted to stop spying. In 1781 Ann and her husband went to England.

When the Continental
Army traveled,
soldiers' families often
went with them.

BIRTH OF A NATION

By September 1783 the fighting was officially over, and the Patriots had won the war. The Americans had been assisted by the French. The French entered the war on the Americans' side in 1779. With their help, the Americans were able to get the British to **surrender** in 1781. In 1783 the Treaty of Paris officially recognized the United States as its own nation.

George Washington was given a hero's welcome in Boston after the Americans won the Revolutionary War.

The brave spies of the Revolutionary War made important contributions to each side's war efforts. The information spies gathered allowed American and British armies to make decisions about how to fight the war. They did this by providing valuable information about troop movements, supplies, and enemy fighting strength. To this day, many historians believe that the Americans' victory was a result of the brave work of their Patriot spies.

surrender—to give up or admit defeat in battle

GLOSSARY

colonist (KAH-luh-nist)—a person who settles in a new territory that is governed by his or her home country, the settled area is called a colony

counterfeit (KOUN-tur-fit)—fake, but looking like the real thing

engraver (en-GRAVE-uhr)—someone who cuts a design or writing into a metal or other hard surface

espionage (ESS-pee-uh-nahzh)—the actions of a spy to gain sensitive national, political, or economic information

intelligence (in-TEL-uh-jenss)—information that can be used to help defeat an enemy

peddler (PED-luhr)—a person who travels around selling things

spy ring (SPYE RING)—a group of spies working together for a common goal

surrender (suh-REN-dur)—to give up or admit defeat in battle

traitor (TRAY-tur)—someone who aids the enemy of his of her country

treason (TREE-zuhn)—the crime of betraying one's country

READ MORE

Gregory, Josh. *The Revolutionary War.* Cornerstones of Freedom. New York: Children's Press, 2012.

Hale, Nathan. *Nathan Hale's Hazardous Tales: One Dead Spy.* New York: Amulet Books, 2012.

Roop, Peter, and Connie Roop. *The Top-Secret Adventure of John Darragh, Revolutionary War Spy.* Minneapolis: Graphic Universe, 2011.

INTERNET SITES

FactHound offers a safe, fun way to find Internet sites related to this book. All of the sites on FactHound have been researched by our staff.

Here's all you do:

Visit *www.facthound.com*

Type in this code: 9781429699778

INDEX

André, John, 18, 19, 20, 21

Arnold, Benedict, 16–21, 39

Bates, Ann, 38–43

Battle of Long Island, 30

Battle of Saratoga, 16

Clinton, Henry, 39, 42

Concord, Massachusetts, 5

Cregge, John, 39

Darragh, Lydia, 22–29

Dawkins, Henry, 8, 11

Fort Ticonderoga, 16

France, 4, 44

Hale, Nathan, 30–37

Hickey, Thomas, 15

Howe, William, 22, 23, 24, 32, 36

Ketcham, Isaac, 8–15

Lexington, Massachusetts, 5

Loyalists, 5, 11, 12, 13, 15, 39

Lynch, Michael, 15

Matthews, David, 15

Patriots, 5, 11, 20, 21, 32, 35, 44, 45

Philadelphia, 8, 11, 17, 22, 24, 26, 28, 29, 39

Scott, Charles, 42

Shippen, Margaret, 17

Washington, George, 6, 11, 15, 16, 19, 22, 24, 26, 30, 37, 39, 42

weapons, 6, 12, 30, 39, 40

West Point, 19, 20

Whitemarsh, 22, 23, 24, 26, 28, 29

Youngs, Isaac, 8, 11

Youngs, Israel, 8, 11